A DARK LIGHT

A DARK LIGHT

NANCY PADDOCK

Teresa Nomura, Artist

VANILLA PRESS
Minneapolis

Two of these poems — "After day's heat," "Snow Goose River," were anthologized in *Women Poets of the Twin Cities*, published by Vanilla Press, 1975. "Yield," "In the mouth of the wolf," "Solar energy," "The mothers," "Estate sale," "Trio for flutes and cello," "Agnes," and "Winter's yield" were first printed in, respectively, *Crazy Horse, Feminist Studies, The North Country Anvil, Oxygen, The Sou'wester, Moons and Lion Tailes, Sing, Heavenly Muse!, and Mainstreeter* (the last two poems), to whose editors I owe thanks for kindly permitting me to include these poems in *A Dark Light*.

Photograph of author (back cover) by Marj Sucoff.

Copyright © 1978 Nancy Paddock

All rights reserved. No part of this book may be reproduced or transmitted for any reason, by any means, without permission in writing from the publisher.

First printing 1978

Library of Congress Catalog Card No.: 77-88047

Paddock, Nancy
   A Dark Light.

Minneapolis, MN: Vanilla Press
72 p.
7710   770907

ISBN 0-917266-13-17

Printed in the United States of America

for Joe

Contents

FUNERALS FOR THE SUN
After day's heat 15
The planting 16
Necrophilia 18
Winter's yield 19
Asleep in Jesus 20
Yield 22
Gross national product 23
The wolves of noon 24
Tides 25

THE MOON'S BEAST
The kindling 29
Two children 30
The pulse of needles 31
The treasure 33
The wedding ring 34
Witch 36
Like my own 37
Phoenix 38
Moontide 39

IN THE CURRENT
Snow Goose River 43
Fireflies 44
The red stone 45
Losing ground 46
Free 47
Trio for flutes and cello 50

CHILD AND MOTHER
Estate sale 55
Lovesong 57
Dream horse 58
Agnes 59
Stigmata 60
The mothers 61
The children come 63
Solar energy 64
Renville County winter 65
The gift 66
In the mouth of the wolf 67
Coming fresh 68

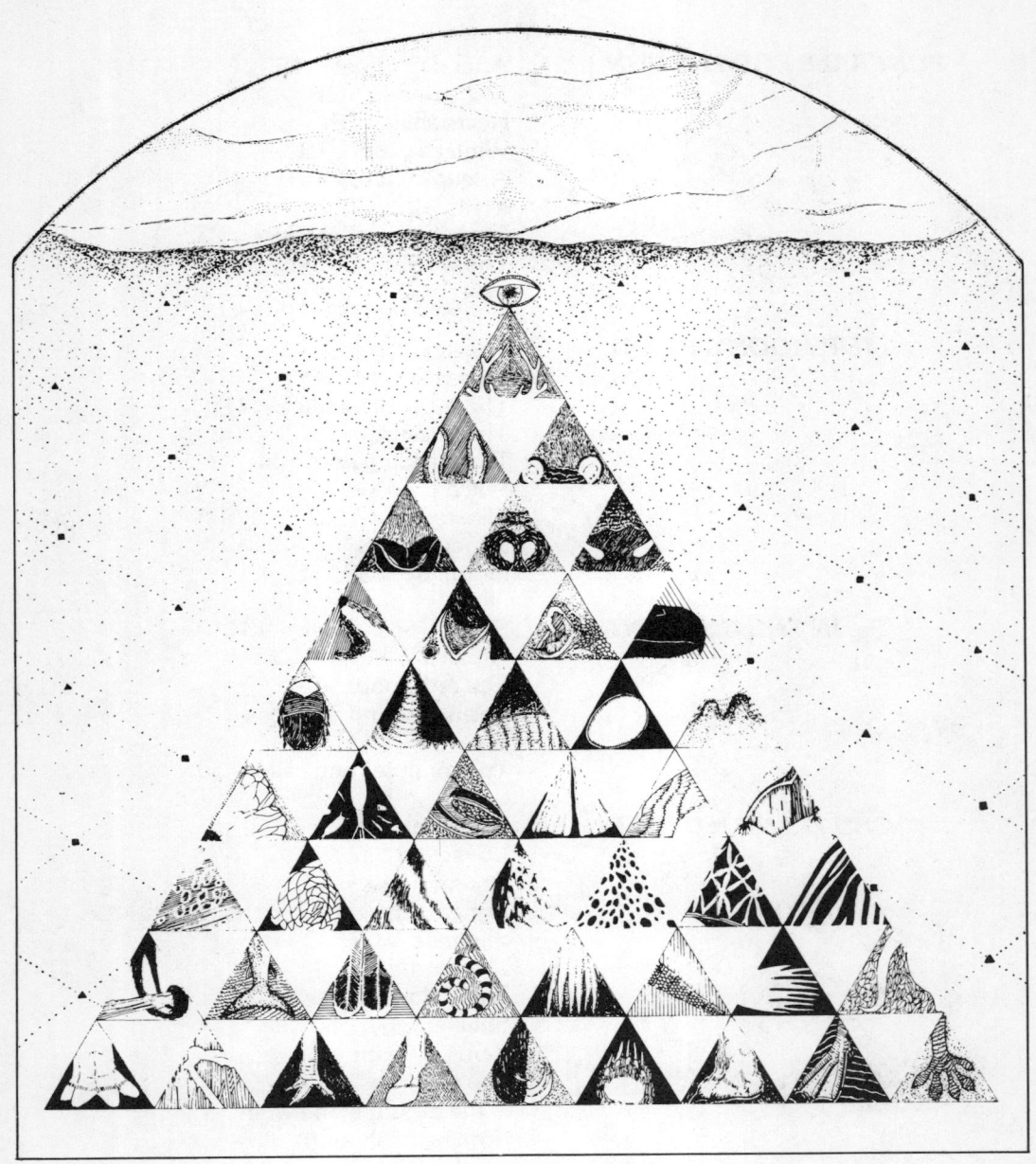

The Gift

A DARK LIGHT

Introduction

"Without our will. . . ." That phrase from one of Nancy Paddock's poems resounds throughout *A Dark Light*. I think of that wonderful but much-maligned word I once heard Nancy use in conversation: submit. Nancy has not been afraid to submit to what difficult truths her dreams have told, to what she has learned from being alone in the woods and from looking long at the everyday lives of the people she lives among. These poems shine with both tenderness and ferocity because Nancy Paddock has been willing to submit to her visions. I am especially struck with how she has faced her own death: She has given herself to it, not with sullen resignation, but with the joyfulness of Whitman. She is not afraid to imagine her skeleton with its "lipless mouth whose kisses swallow time." Nor does she hesitate to see her body in the ground and to draw us into her marvelous litany ending: "let field mice nibble calcium from my hand /and young/plants swell my hips/wasps give my body wings."

    Nancy Paddock's poems belie what some critics say about women poets: that they cannot write well about nature. The nature Nancy writes of here is frequently fierce — but it is also lush and benevolent, as in "After day's heat": "in gardens/radishes split/and by the roadside/soft dusty raspberries fall." When she comes out of her solitude to write about people, she transforms their common lives and makes us see them more clearly. In these poems we live with the rituals of wedding showers, country auctions, funerals, planting gardens, making quilts, and there is a luminescence even in the loneliness of Agnes chopping wood for the kitchen woodstove: "that land sustaining you through work/that sprouted green from your hands." I'm glad Nancy Paddock ends *A Dark Light* with the poem "Coming fresh." All the elements of her work come together in this last poem to leave us with the radiance of the wonderful sense that we have come through a dark birth ourselves:

> The priceless body.
> The mystery.
> The transformation of the grass
> into new flesh.

— Phebe Hanson

FUNERALS FOR THE SUN

Asleep in Jesus

AFTER DAY'S HEAT

after day's heat
the slow gray summer twilight
a growing silence
    cricket
      distant hum of bees
    wasps   still working against dark

hardly a birdsong all day
in buzzing fields of yellow, purple, white

in gardens   radishes split
and by the roadside
soft dusty raspberries   fall

and now
a night breeze through birch leaves
a whippoorwill
the dark

in the weight of a waxing moon
across the full river
the wail of young wolves
is winter

THE PLANTING

for Camilla Hall

on my knees
beneath the shadow of a cloud
I dig a furrow with my hands
where earthworms eat their way
among roots and the good dead

Camilla Hall is dead
in love-starved America
those who will not let us forget
are blown away

feed my sheep

I remember her   a self-conscious kid in the fifties
boyish and brilliant
how does a woman   the minister's daughter
last of his seed
find herself
a Joan of Arc?

seeds fall into the ground
and die

this is my body

and she abideth   alone

this is my blood shed

and did she fire
or no fire
burn to the end?

I crumble soft earth over seeds
and wait for rain

and the strange fruit
of storms

NECROPHILIA

I live with death
watching the years line up and sink
into my face   my body
sending messages of death   a skeleton
lover that lies
beside me
the naked jaw in profile
on that other pillow
in my grave

I stare into eyes that open
into darkness
a lipless mouth whose kisses
swallow time

I wake from eucharists of rotten meat
believing I am old

afraid to die
because life is a door
I have not opened
a half life in a dim room
half gone

afraid to live because death
is a door that opens
itself

my nights   a marriage
feast of bones

my days   a procession
of funerals
for the sun

WINTER'S YIELD

for Bill Holm

the old Icelandic Lutheran Church
is closed
but the cemetery is open
to the high prairie wind
and visitors who break   ice
off the old iron gate

each withered blade of grass is closed
in ice   thick
as thumbs
and fingers   reaching up
crunch underfoot
with the sound of teeth
on salmon bones

alive   unbreathing
within its tomb of ice
an elm bows to the ground
and breaks
bearing winter's yield
like clusters of ripe apples

only the gravestones with stern Icelandic names
Thorgrimson   Gottskalksson
stand firm
unyielding and preserved forever
in frozen shields

and choked with ice
the throat of a plastic rose
is closed
as an eye
long turned to dust

ASLEEP IN JESUS

the old cemetery at Morton   the final
resting place of pioneers
after they had broken
the sod
thrust their roots into the tangled
web of ancient grass

a tree   carved from pale sandstone
a leafless monument   bearing
only words
an amputated stump
of loss unbending
the family tree

its branches scattered on the ground
like bones
with the names of children:

       Daniel   born 1881
               died 1893

and Benjamin   1884 to 1902

   "Asleep in Jesus, blessed sleep,
   From which none wakes to weep."

awake, unweeping Gunder Lind dug stones
that worked up in his wheat fields
every spring   for thirty years
dug stones and buried
sons
till he had plowed the prairie
black   opening
its darkness to the wind
carving deep   his grief:

*"'Tis hard to break the tender cord
When love has bound the heart.
'Tis hard, so hard, to speak the words,
Must we forever part?
Dearest loved one, we have laid thee
In the peaceful grave's embrace,
But thy memory will be cherished
Till we see thy heavenly face."*

*"O blessed sleep
from which none wakes . . ."*

at fifty-two, unyielding Gunder Lind
fell down
weary of the hardness he bore
out of the ground

tears still break
out of these stones
washing down the furrowed names
dissolving
even the hardest

leaving this tree
that they may not go
unmarked   into the ground
these pioneers
who dropped their seed
into the darkness
and bore
its fruit

YIELD

they worked the land together
his grain fields and her garden
forty years
of children and pickles
tomato juice put by
potatoes and squash in the cellar

always the planting and the harvest
gangs of young men   red
and hungry at her table
the steaming woodstove

now her garden is grown up
in weeds
and the dark stalks
of last year's sunflowers
bow their heads
no longer bending with the days

and he is enveloped
in the roar of his machine
slowly sowing
acres of identical seeds

GROSS NATIONAL PRODUCT

thin house   stripped and empty
squatting
awkward in a field of wheat
that springs right up to the door
wheat   small and green
as a lawn
a flat sea spreading
road to road

an elm sapling leaps
out of the shadow of the house
gripping
the only stones unturned
where bare ditchbanks
cut
straight as meridian lines
across sprayed fields
and county roads   laid
over the features of the land
become a graph
plotting profit

and loss

THE WOLVES OF NOON

cicada buzzsaw whines
along the jawbone
its tangible hymn
to the day

steam wavers
over a horizon of dried corn
at the edge of town
a corridor of dust
tracks a picker down the rows

summer is played out   swollen
cabbages   fat and yellow
cucumbers on shriveled vines
a robin listens
to the hard ground
as the noon whistle screams
downtown   a wolf
that ate the morning
and the chewed bones of afternoon
spread out to dry
in the heat

retreating
into the shimmer above asphalt
everything changes
into something else

this house becomes a clock
day after day   identical
and monotonous
as the heartbeat
its shadow slowly circles
with empty hands

TIDES

1

night lives   within the bodies
of all animals
the sinking sun
draws shadows out of them
as song

quivering of a thousand crickets
fluting of the thrush
release
the mantra of a whippoorwill

night is breathing
in the throats of frogs
hooing owls
with moonrise
brush wolves' voices
slide
among the lunar fluids
of our cells

2

song rises before the sun
light
from the breasts of birds
calling the sun to them
pulls day
out of our sleep
ending the dark hunt

THE MOON'S BEAST

The Pulse of Needles

THE KINDLING

moon inflamed
nibbled at the edge
rising with heat lightning

stars sear holes in trees
fireflies singe the wind

this cabin   closed
against a night on fire
moths beating screens for light
mosquitoes hanging
humming in our heat

in the dark valley
brush wolves wail   burning
for the moon

TWO CHILDREN

two corpses
without flesh
hands of small bones clasped
in hard intimacy
two children

find me the book behind the dream
the child
line of her throat marked
for the knife
and her brother dead
within his mother's gaze
the fluid of his veins
turned solid

I sent this boy from my door
and when I saw
at the crossroads   the girl child
and her auburn horse
come silently to me
I hurried on   aware
of a weak wish to hold them
and my fear

THE PULSE OF NEEDLES

wedding quilts for all her sisters
young brothers
quilt-wrapped when they come of age
the satin christening coverlets
for every godchild
keep her lap full

and she is caught up
in her sewing
when each loved one has been covered
by her silent song

she never married
she chose a soft geometry
refusing the children
that would have left her
refusing the hardness
of a man

her time
is measured in no hours or seasons
she marks instead
the pulse of needles
threading through the days
her body
focused on that point
achieves a distance
a hibernation
in the jaws of life

but in her dream
red blood   drops
into her lap
from where the needle pierces
cloth

cloth that cushions
insulates against the cold
patterns that break
the fevers of beds
cover them over with ordered shapes
to hide the dying

stars
that do not burn
flowers that never seed
or drop their petals

THE TREASURE

the jeweled maidens flow solemnly
to their lovers   waiting long
and thirsting
in the grave's mouth

virgins   so willing
to be married
to this softening flesh
to be carried
in arms   dark red and shining
to be buried   alive
seeds
mated to the ground

their children
will be ground water
and the springing grain

THE WEDDING RING

hair cut short
soft-bodied   face still
innocent as your children
you are the brown bird
watching
your mate's display

he struts
grows sideburns   a mustache
he wears white shoes and smokes a thin cigar
believes in God
and Motherhood

and you
dream of piercing
your ears
and dancing the tango
in jangling silver chains

you wear
the confirmation pearls
your mother gave you
but your sleep is full
of wolves
snapping at your feet

a gray horse
without a rider   calling:
"Come!
Run with me through the wild dawn —
where scarlet blossoms rip
to drop blood fruit,
and trees snare the moon
in their long fingers."

and in your dream
your husband cuts your nose off
and you snatch it up
and paste it on your face

it stays
but there will always be
the thin red mark

a ring
around it

WITCH

small town on the Minnesota prairie
young matron   awake
through the hot night
naked   in dark rooms
her white body gleaming

she knows she is invisible now
in garments of darkness
crouching in a chair
stares out a window at the moon
alone   and sovereign
for this time

then scrambles undercover
as the sky pales
and moths held all night
in the arc of a streetlamp
are released

LIKE MY OWN

for Joe

rain   cold across your cheek
lifts me into singing

the forest flickering   on your face
green and strange as spring
leaves me lost
alone

I know your body like my own

I hear the call of winds
beneath your voice

your eyes   dark lairs
of gentle beasts
warmblooded
wild

the open door of music in your smile
leaves honey
in my darkness
softens stone

I love your body

like my own

PHOENIX

this old house is closed forever
doors nailed across windows
blistering paint
blank stretches along eaves
that used to swirl with gingerbread

flames have eaten the stairway to my rooms
opening walls
to the wind

the elm tree is burned black
on one side
but the other is still green

here where I saw the red sun
of my future   rise
through black steel gates

and I knew a death
the burning
pain of birth

MOONTIDE

lying long awake   full
of the moon
eyes pulled open
beneath that blind face

mirror of love and dread
goddess   cold
though swept by fire of stars

tides of cold light
in my flesh   ebbing from earth
to that bright desert
sister
dark brilliance
touching my core

and I know I am the moon's beast
lifted   to rest in her
within my blood's heat

IN THE CURRENT

Trio for Flutes and Cello

SNOW GOOSE RIVER

all night they pass
under the sinking moon
following the bright Missouri
from Sand Lake and the snow

joy-cries in the cold
and coyotes answer
beneath Orion's wheel   hunting
until dawn

with light
honeying their wings
snow geese are waves
of the pale sky

they circle
a slow spiraling galaxy
sucked down into the same slough
thousands and thousands
of geese and years

a current
deep as their blood
drawn by summer across the world
their bodies   in flight
outline the shifting mountains
of the air

FIREFLIES

the black air flashes with stars
hissing into the river

drawn to earth   by desire
out of the great valley
of the Milky Way

darkness is one
river
deep as an eye
round   unblinking
looking into me

and I see
lights
rise and swim out
on burning wings

THE RED STONE

as a child I found a stone and kept it
smooth and red
four dark planets   still
within its secret
mine

lost
somewhere for years
last night in a dream
I found it   glistening
a living cell
cupped in a white-haired woman's hands

I touched the dark star-center
and it was
my own

LOSING GROUND

willows shaking silver
long grass tossing in the wind
the river   cold
pulled always downward   and away

past sandbars   log jams
trees undercut
and grasping with bare fingers
their dark hair
roots   snarled in earth

drawing out my breath
stealing sand beneath my feet
the current   stronger than
my body is heavy

letting go

I am carried
in dark arms of the river

to drift
and drown
in sunlight

FREE

White walls draped with Bicentennial flags,
cracked Liberty Bell,
and star-spangled copies of the Declaration.
The Minneota Manor,
room after room of clean beds
with tiny bodies,
embryonic,
curling toward deliverance.

Two framed photographs in the hall,
before and after,
captioned: "Anna Thorson,
Outstanding —
because of her years."
A solemn bride in 1910, full
fleshed as a peach.
Consumed now
to the essential stone,
crumpled in a wheelchair, playing with her dress.

A hundred people pushed
into the dining room, before we arrived.
Wheelchairs and walkers,
beds cranked up.
We read
as a woman loudly asks her mother,
"Can you hear? They're reading poems!"
She mumbles, "What?
No . . . I don't know . . . ,"
and looks away.

Clouded smiles, applause,
attendants serving coffee and juice.

Strapped in his chair,
a thin man with a mustache elegantly
nibbles a paper napkin —
meticulously
unscrews the cap from a sugar container
and fills his cup.

Then Bill starts to play
and Roy's harmonica joins in:
> *"You are my sunshine, my only sunshine,*
> *You make me happy, when skies are gray . . ."*

Lips find the words.
A blank-faced woman
taps the table with one finger.
Old Charlie Munson slumps in his chair,
and doesn't wipe the tears.

And the years,
freely spilled as water,
flow back to a barn dance
of sweat and swirling skirts.
He's up and dancing:
> *"Roll out the barrel,*
> *We'll have a barrel of fun.*
> *Roll out the barrel,*
> *We've got the blues on the run.*
> *Zing boom ta-ra-ra!*
> *Sing out a song of good cheer!*
> *Now's the time to roll the barrel,*
> *For the gang's all here."*

Schottisch, two-step, polka, waltz,
the circle of bodies,
unbroken,
in his eyes.
But he is blind to the old woman,
floating, here, on the music,
lips slightly parted, arms reaching out,
her fingers cupping the shoulder
of a ghost.

"*Let Me Call You Sweetheart*,"
"*I Want a Girl*,"
"*Bye-bye Blackbird*," and it's over.
Bill tells Charlie, "We'll be back,"
and Charlie's eyes narrow
as he grins through his teeth:

"You're damned right!
All we get in this place
is church stuff!"

Out in the yard, he sets out
alone
toward a stubblefield,
and Bill whispers, "Let him go."

But even when a nurse leads Charlie
back by the hand,
I see him dancing.
Side-stepping a haze of years
and tranquilizers,
slipping all the kind hands.

His solitary polka
spinning out a joy
that is free.

"You're damned right!"

TRIO FOR FLUTES AND CELLO

two girls with honey-colored hair
play Haydn
their faces a lake at dawn
reflect the quiet sky
their flutesong floats
     the bouncing flight of wrens
     or child gymnasts   slipping
     through steel bars
     without the weight of years

a lovely woman
plays the cello between them
her face transparent to the deep
springs that feed her
and the dark
voice of the cello beats
     wild wings
     of a black swan

this music is a flickering   of sun
and shadow on new leaves
a cord   forming itself
from singing streams
it binds blossom scent
to sweet juice
of apple on the tongue

the girls are new   waiting
for magic to come
out of them
they blow chaste kisses   over the mouths
of silver rivers

but the woman has sunk
into the current
has cut through to the heart
with her bow
she opens
the full body of the cello
and brings forth

a dark light

CHILD AND MOTHER

Dream Horse

ESTATE SALE

the furniture of her life
spread over the yard for strangers
eyes   and fingers
feel for something solid
some thread
from the whole cloth
of the past

polished brass bed
the heavy oak table and buffet
her best china
Red Wing crocks   boxes
of clouded zinc-capped Mason jars

all for sale
all drowning
in the quick litany
of the auctioneer:

   "What'll ya give me?"

he picks through sheets and towels
with crocheted edges
grabs up an armload of quilt:

   "What do I hear? A dollar?
   C'mon, do I hear two?"

for more than a hundred hours of work

I can't resist
bid ten dollars to take home
the pieces of a life   bound together
a patchwork
of tiny-flowered baby clothes

splashy apron paisleys
tired blue stripes of a husband's pajamas

a pattern of her own   created
with patience
of the slow silent mending
of wounds

women's work
made to be used   worn out
to keep us warm

because my mother   and my grandmother
did not make quilts
I'll sleep tonight
beneath the stitches of a stranger
who sleeps
beneath the ground
and the thread   unbroken
passes on to me

LOVESONG

for Jennifer Langham

her body   tautly tuned
enfolds the cello
fingers measuring the limits
of the strings
weaving webs
of melody that hold us
over an abyss
of silence

she rocks
the cello like a child
or lover   sounding
the depths of sound
and surfacing
with harmony in her soul's shape

the heart's music
playing over her face   like wind
over water
and she is in the throes of giving
life   to twin worlds
or moons
behind her eyelids

she draws
her bow over our bones
quickening marrow
and the dry wood
of the cello sprouts green
song
that lives again

DREAM HORSE

nine nights without sleep
my spine   a column of fists
refusing to let go
but sinking   at last
out of weakness
into the dream chamber
of the gray mare

tame
greeting me as though my own
only as tall as I   she comes
too close
dark eyes   warm breath on my face

lifting a hoof   soft and unshod
she presses my thigh
with firm gentle weight
I sink   slowly
to the ground
unable to free myself

heavy forelegs
muscled and warm
dappled gray hair
over my legs   my arms

I know helplessness
stillness
rest

dream horse   come
reclaim me
bring me home

child and mother of my deepest valley
ride me

AGNES

Agnes   old woman   alone
all the children were afraid of you
your hands curved in upon themselves
like bird claws that would not open
even for love
cradling an ax
your thin arms chopped wood
for the old blue kitchen woodstove
you carried buckets in the crook of your elbow

I see you brushing brown hair from your eyes
with swollen knuckles
faded cotton dress stretched across your bones
bent always   over work

you were always there
I climbed your tree to my refuge
my throne
and below you listened   taking
all my grade school loves and hurt
seriously
I was the only child you ever had

in all our talk   only once
you cracked your smoldering world for me
a battleground   for God and Satan
the mere four thousand souls to be released
you wanted to let me in
to that Beulahland
behind your small bright eyes

that land sustaining you through work
that sprouted green from your hands
and nights   shades pulled
in a house with closed-off rooms
of pain

STIGMATA

swollen with child   her body
stretched on the beating frame
of love's continual making

she could only wait and yield
to its time
an engine of dreadful grace

now her stretchmarked belly
is a soft empty fruit
its seed
delivered up

THE MOTHERS

they are old now
with quiet eyes
hands still
soft arms and breasts falling
empty   to their laps
in loose flowered dresses
they lean toward each other
almost whispering

this is my wedding shower
I am a girl
to them   and I almost forget
my more than thirty years
we are stranger
to each other   than we know
and yet they gather
a circle
of gifts and blessings
to welcome me   because
I am a wife
a daughter

the old mothers   wishing children
into my belly
wishing me safe journey
 on the ancient path   worn
  deep   by slow feet

they do what everybody does
they bear
their husbands' names
first and last
and children   caught
in photographs
the son's jutting chin and narrow eyes

the daughter
pale lips smiling from her frame

Mrs. Howard ("Howie") Pederson
Mrs. Calvin T. Johnson
they smile and take my hand
and I feel their lives
flow into mine

one plays the organ   stumbling   carefully
finding
her own harmony
"*Bless this house . . .*"   they pray
for me
and I could weep

the mothers   their lives
are a never-ending chain
of love
of children
and their children's children

springing out of their arms

THE CHILDREN COME

I dreamed of a child
her headless skeleton
burned brown

my mother laid this body
bones stretched out
upon my bones

I woke up sobbing:
"What am I
to do with her?"

the children come   no matter what
the world is doing
they are born
to starving mothers   dead
or unknown fathers
they are borne

out of the prolonged labor
of war   sucking
dry breasts
and dying   they are born

SOLAR ENERGY

getting in wood from the old pile of birch
split and curling
darkened with three years of weather
the unsplit lengths   spongy
inside bark cylinders
smelling of soil
sprouting seashells   delicate ruffles   fungus ears
with smooth cool skin

in this chill November of no desire
the earth is dark
with death   light
shines through
empty forms of sloughed snakeskins
stillness rushes in veins
of dry leaves   shed
as deer shed antlers

gravity is love
of the Mother for her children
the soil   her embrace
a darkness remaining
behind all changes
full of light

this woodpile
sunfire locked in cells
will be released
into the ground
or enter my body
as warmth and light
my mind

RENVILLE COUNTY WINTER

it is the nakedness
that hurts
the eyes
pry into things
which should be covered

defoliated fields   gray
as a cracked lakebottom
ripple to a flat horizon
where islands
of bare trees   expose
farmyards to the sky

an unfinished drainage ditch
cuts
like a battle line
strung with broken bones
of tile

and the graves of all that died
into the soil
are robbed
by the light
fingers of the wind

THE GIFT

without our will
we find ourselves   like grass
reaching out of the ground

swallowing bodies
of animals and plants
we merge with them

nothing is our own

plant me naked under fallen leaves in spring
let maggots waken in my flesh
let beetles open out my eyes
lay eggs along my grinning teeth

let field mice nibble calcium from my hand
and young
plants swell my hips

wasps   give my body wings

IN THE MOUTH OF THE WOLF

I howl
mocking her from a tree
and then I fall
(it was my secret wish
to fall)

and cower in a corner
where she stands over me
a gray shadow with golden eyes

the wolf takes my hand
in her teeth
opening my flesh until blood flows
into the warm darkness
of her
soft mouth

nursing my wound
she is a child suckling
she is a fierce
and gentle mother
I feed

with my own blood
she heals me

COMING FRESH

We walk out on Christmas Day
from table talk: the price
of feed and milk,
worthless beef,
to watch pale light fade off the snow.

A willow's brittle arc
is amber
as we wander toward the barn.

The rigid body
of a young bull
lies where he dropped in the yard.

Judy tells how cats ate
a stillborn calf,
points out the sore on the bull's knee
that brought him down.

We enter the sweet smell
of damp hay and manure,
the dark barn warmed
by the bodies   of cows.
A double row of warm machines,
with swelling udders,   giving
gallons and gallons.

Jaws grind. Dung
slops in the gutter.
Thick tails switch the walk
where cats step carefully.
In dark corners,
green heads of half-wild mallards,
in for the winter against wolves.

Then sudden crossed white hooves
reach out of the mother.

The cow lies in straw,
head still locked in the stanchions,
distended belly rising
and falling.
Relaxed in the rhythm
of the yearly creation   of milk
and meat.

She bears down
and the nose comes, tongue lolling,
enveloped in translucent film.
But the big collie sniffs too close.
She bellows, contracts,
sucks the calf back into her.

The ancient fear of teeth.

John drives the dog away
and slips a noose of twine
around the calf's small hooves.
A slow expert pull,
the inexorable push.
Urine splatters into the gutter behind us.
And the calf slides out
like a wound spilling
guts into the dirt.

Alive.

Alone.
Slimy and whole.

He blinks into the half-light,
snuffling to clear his lungs,
lifting his head.

The priceless body.
The mystery.
The transformation of the grass
into new flesh.

Our warmth
in this winter,
coming fresh.

Renville County Winter

Photo by Gerry Zeck

Teresa Nomura is a Minneapolis-born-and-raised artist. She studied painting at the University of Minnesota and is currently making mixed-media, soft-sculptured environments. Whether with pen or needle in hand, she expresses the intangible fantasy/reality of every day.